Michelle

By **Deborah Hopkinson**   Illustrated by **AG Ford**

KATHERINE TEGEN BOOKS
An Imprint of HarperCollins Publishers

For Michele Hill, who has always
helped others to dream big
—D.H.

To my loving sisters, Nicola and Erica
—A.F.

Katherine Tegen Books is an imprint of HarperCollins Publishers.

Michelle
Text copyright © 2009 by Deborah Hopkinson
Illustrations copyright © 2009 by AG Ford

Library of Congress Cataloging-in-Publication Data
Hopkinson, Deborah.
Michelle / by Deborah Hopkinson ; Illustrated by A.G. Ford. — 1st ed.
p. cm.
ISBN 978-0-06-182739-6 (trade bdg.) — ISBN 978-0-06-182743-3 (lib. bdg.)
1. Obama, Michelle, 1964-—Juvenile literature. 2. Presidents' spouses—United States—
Biography—Juvenile literature. 3. Legislators' spouses—United States—Biography—Juvenile
literature. 4. African American women lawyers—Illinois—Chicago—Biography—Juvenile
literature. 5. Chicago (Ill.)—Biography—Juvenile literature I. Ford,
A. G., ill. II. Title.
E909.O24H66 2009   973.932092—dc22   [B]   2009014551   CIP   AC

Typography by Rachel Zegar
09 10 11 12 13 CG/WORZ 10 9 8 7 6 5 4 3 2 1
❖
First Edition

Michelle Robinson Obama became First Lady of the United States on January 20, 2009, just three days after her forty-fifth birthday.

On that historic inauguration day, Michelle's husband, Barack Obama, took the oath of office, pledging to lead the nation into a new birth of freedom.

By his side stood Michelle, smart and sure. Michelle, proud wife and mother, loving daughter, sister, and friend, an ordinary girl who grew up to do extraordinary things.

This is her story.

Michelle was born in the heart of winter, on the
South Side of Chicago.

Chicago can be a cold, windy place, but Michelle's
parents, Fraser and Marian, made a warm and loving
home for their baby girl and her big brother, Craig.

Fraser Robinson was proud that his job operating pumps at the city water plant could support his family. Michelle knew how hard her dad worked and looked up to him from the time she was little. Even after she got big, Michelle loved to sit on his lap, resting her head on his shoulder.

Marian Robinson believed in education and taught Craig and Michelle to read by the time they were four. Since homework came first, she was strict about television: just an hour a day. But Michelle still managed to memorize whole episodes of her favorite show, *The Brady Bunch*.

From her father, Michelle learned courage. She watched him go to work cheerfully each day, even after he developed multiple sclerosis, a disease that made it hard for him to walk.

From her mother, Michelle learned to ask questions—to *think*. Her mom taught her to believe in herself, to learn from mistakes, to follow her heart—and to get things done.

From both her parents, Michelle learned to dream big.

Michelle's parents hadn't been to college, but they wanted their children to have that chance.

Saving for education came first, even if it meant they lived simply, in a one-bedroom apartment on Euclid Avenue. They divided the living room to make separate spaces for Michelle and Craig, with a small, shared area for reading and studying.

The Robinsons might not have had a fancy house, but they had one another. The family ate dinner together at night (Michelle loved macaroni and cheese). They enjoyed reading and playing games—Monopoly, Chinese checkers, and card games.

But Craig had to watch out. That spunky little sister he called Miche sure loved to beat him!

That was Michelle. As her mom always said, Michelle wanted to be the best.

Going away to college might have seemed a big dream for
a working-class girl from the South Side.

But Michelle knew how to stick with things, whatever it
took. And she never gave up.

From the time she was little, Michelle worked hard at
school, even skipping second grade. In sixth grade, she
entered a special class for gifted students. She graduated
from eighth grade as salutatorian—second in her class.

Her hard work earned Michelle a place at one of the best

schools in Chicago, Whitney M. Young Magnet High School. It
meant a long trip each way—an hour and a half ride, morning
and night. But Michelle didn't complain; she just studied on the
bus. And she made the honor roll each year.

    When it came time to apply to college, Michelle aimed high.
No matter what anyone said, she made up her mind that if
her big brother could be accepted at Princeton, one of the top
universities in the country, so could she.

    And she was.

Michelle did well at Princeton University. But sometimes, on campus, in a sea of white faces, she wondered if a South Side girl like her really belonged.

Michelle wondered, too, where her path—and her dreams—would take her next.

Eager to keep learning, Michelle went on
to graduate from Harvard Law School.

Then she returned home to Chicago for
her first job as a lawyer.

At the law firm, she was asked to advise a Harvard law student who had been hired for the summer. His name was Barack Obama.

Barack seemed to know right away that Michelle was the one for him. He urged her to give him a chance, winning her over with a visit to the Art Institute of Chicago, a movie, and best of all, ice cream. He made her laugh and drove her around in his old car with a hole in the floor.

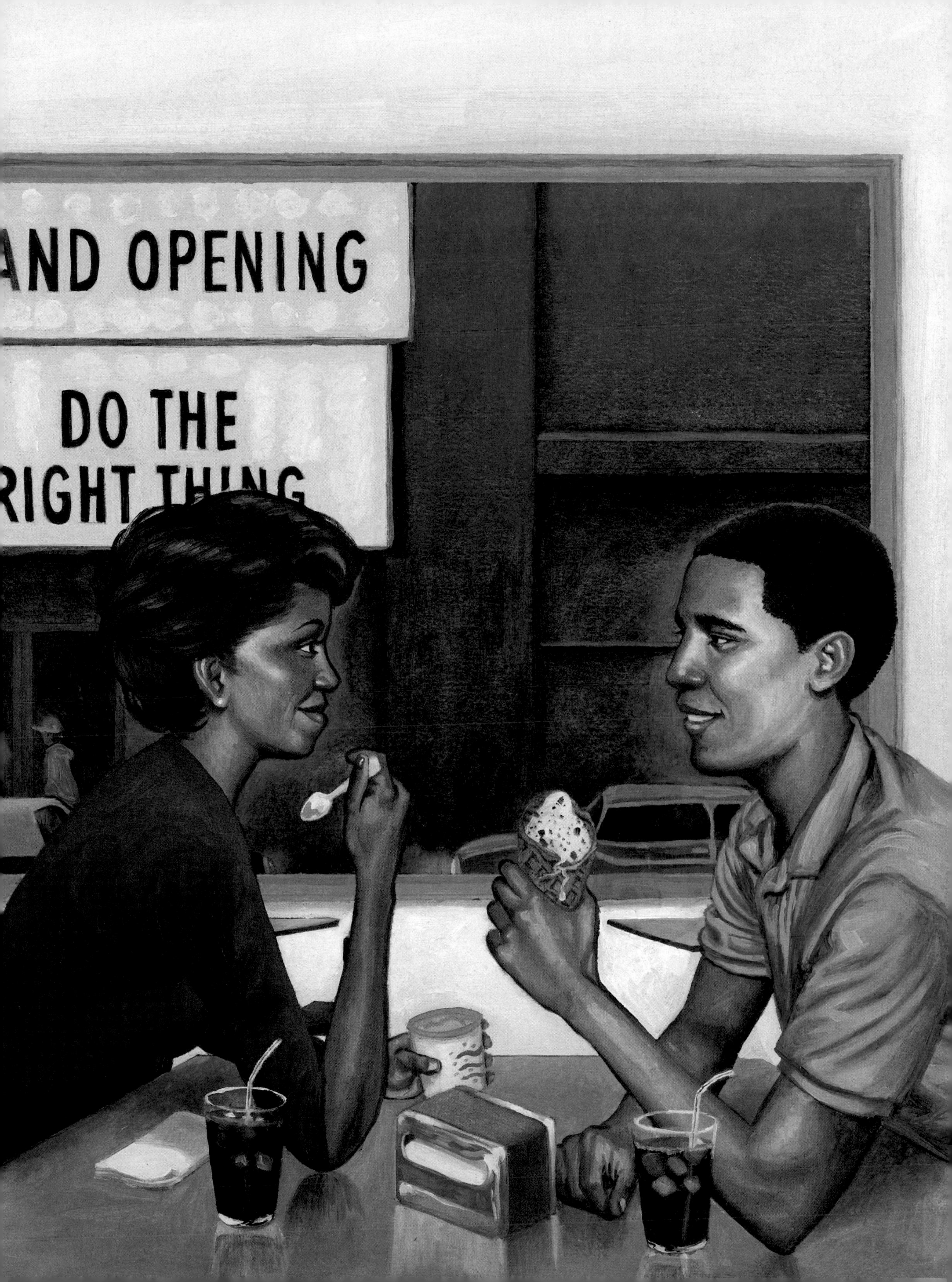
AND OPENING
DO THE
RIGHT

But mostly he won her heart by sharing his vision of hope and change. Michelle fell in love, realizing there was something special about this handsome young man with the unusual name.

Barack proposed to Michelle at a fancy restaurant. To Michelle's surprise, the engagement ring arrived with dessert!

Michelle and Barack were married on October 3, 1992.

Michelle's mom and brother were at her wedding. But her dad had died in 1991.

Michelle's dad had always encouraged her to give back. And about this time Michelle decided to make a big change: she left the law firm to work in community service.

Down-to-earth, bright, and practical, Michelle had always been able to get things done. Now she used her talents to take on some big, important jobs.

She trained young community leaders, encouraged university students to volunteer, and helped improve health care for families on Chicago's South Side.

Michelle loved her new work and succeeded at whatever she set out to do. She realized that working for others was what she wanted most. She was living her own dreams by making things better for the community she loved.

Michelle had another dream too—to be a mother. Malia was born in 1998 and Sasha in 2001. Michelle and Barack devoted themselves to being good parents to their daughters.

When the girls were little, Barack was often gone, serving in the Illinois State Senate in Springfield. That sometimes made it hard for Michelle to balance her own job with being a mom.

But when things got tough, Michelle found a way
to get things done. She made plans and got organized.
She turned to her mother, who was always there when
Michelle needed her, for help and support. Marian
Robinson loved picking up the girls from school and
being a big part of their lives.

And of course, Malia and Sasha helped, too, by
making their beds and doing their chores!

Michelle had sometimes wondered if politics was the best way to make things better. Yet she realized Barack was a true leader—the kind America needed.

So Michelle worked to help Barack run for the United States Senate. When he got the chance to make a speech to the whole nation, Barack's words of hope and change electrified people everywhere. Soon he was off to Washington, D.C., as a new senator.

Sometimes, dreams take us places we never imagine.

Just a couple of years later, under a bright cold winter sky, Michelle found herself beside Barack at the Old State Capitol in Springfield, Illinois.

There, where Abraham Lincoln had once stood to speak, Barack Obama announced that he would run for president.

In the long, hard months that followed, millions of people across the country took up Barack's rallying cry of change: "Yes, we can!"

While Malia and Sasha stayed home with their grandmother, Michelle made short trips to help Barack campaign, speaking to crowds large and small.

Michelle spoke about possibilities—of her own dreams as a girl from a working-class family and the confidence her parents had given her to make good choices.

Michelle spoke of how each child in America deserved a chance to excel and of the need to make life better for struggling families.

Michelle listened too.

She listened as people shared their fears and hopes—and their trust that Barack could bring all Americans together.

And then the people voted.

They were old and young, women and men.
They came from farms and cities, from small
towns and mountain villages, from islands and
deserts. They were of many races and religions.
They were Americans.

On November 4, 2008, Barack Obama was elected the forty-fourth president of the United States.

Michelle and Barack had made history.
And on this night of new beginnings, Michelle stood ready to keep working hard, to help her own children, and children and families across America, make their big dreams come true.

And so it was that on January 20, 2009,
inauguration night, all eyes turned to her—
tall and graceful, bold and beautiful,
Michelle Obama, First Lady of America.

Author's Note

Michelle LaVaughn Robinson Obama was born on January 17, 1964. She grew up in the small upstairs apartment of a brick bungalow on the South Side of Chicago with her parents, Marian and Fraser Robinson III, and her older brother, Craig.

Bright and hard-working, Michelle was always an outstanding student. In 1981, she graduated from Whitney M. Young Magnet High School, where she was a member of the National Honor Society. She received her bachelor's degree from Princeton University in 1985 and a J.D. from Harvard Law School in 1988.

After law school, Michelle returned to Chicago to work for the firm of Sidley & Austin, where she met Barack Obama. Michelle chose to stop practicing law for a career focused on community service. In 1993, she became executive director of Public Allies, a nonprofit organization that prepares young adults for careers in community work and social change. In 1996, she joined the University of Chicago, where she developed the university's community service center, which encourages students to become volunteers.

In 2002, Michelle became executive director for community affairs for the University of Chicago Medical Center. Her leadership and accomplishments in improving community-based health care for citizens on the South Side of Chicago led to her promotion to vice president for community and external affairs in 2005.

Michelle married Barack Obama on October 3, 1992. Michelle is a devoted mother to the couple's two daughters, Malia, born on July 4, 1998, and Sasha, born on June 10, 2001. In addition to having her own career, Michelle has helped Barack in his work. She played an especially important role in his successful campaign for president, inspiring men, women, and children with her direct, down-to-earth humor and personal story of hard work and success.

Michelle Obama can trace her family's roots back many years, to when America was a very different place. Her great-great-grandfather Jim Robinson was born around 1850 and was enslaved on a South Carolina plantation. On inauguration day 2009, Michelle Obama became America's first African American First Lady.